The Mad Tales

Pi Kielty

KAPHEIRA
PRESS

Cover photo: "Above the Clouds II"
Courtesy of Craig Mueller

ISBN 978-0692504079

DEDICATION

This book is dedicated to the memory of the late Syd Barrett, founder of the Pink Floyd. May all of our Mad Cap Laughs turn out better than his.

THE TALES

INTRODUCTION TO THE
SECOND EDITION

While trekking through the jungles of Borneo, sweat soaking the brim of my hat, I stopped to rest at the base of a waterfall. From out of the forest walked Pi Kielty. Our introduction was a bit startling as he'd been living amongst a group of Wild Men for the previous month and was a bit worse for wear. Turns out, he needed a break from his previous career attempting to be the foremost African small game hunter in the world. He figured that everyone could hunt the big five. His outfit emphasized the small seven. In hindsight, there were a few issues with that business model. Then there was the attempt to summit near each of the seven highest peaks on each continent. Not the highest peaks, mind you, but the one located to the left of each one. Left being a rather arbitrary measurement. At least no one had accomplished that yet. It would be one for the record books. The man sure knew how to live, though. A tattered knapsack with a couple books, some instant coffee and a carton of camels. The experience was what mattered. The Mad Tales was born from this spirit.

Craig Mueller - August 2015

PI KIELTY

Forward
Alternative Realism and The Auto-Horrific

I once had pretty imaginative ideas, long ago. These ideas even preceded, and in some cases later, exceeded my experiences with hallucinations on drugs. Most times, imagination never translates well into writing. With much gratitude, I gave up completely all mind-altering recreation years ago. Only then was I able to do my humble attempt to formulate my imagination into a form of literature that I call "alternative realism and the auto-horrific." To my great disappointment, I feel that even with a story that tickles my thalamus (part of that "un-scratchable itch" from *Quixote of River City*), I never come close to blowing anyone else's mind the way my own would explode in the mushroom cloud of perception from my natural paranoid state of mind. Still, I still go by that old hippie guru axiom: Never completely trust an artist who never gimped out on psilocybin.

Only clear thoughts would later give me some

such idea as alternative realism. The experience of a poisoned mind brought me to the auto-horrific. The ideas came about, like ideas come to other authors, through experience in life, but even more from the influence of art and the artists who made it. While I can claim no magistry like artist whose influence I claim, they did and still do help form my mind for my work and give it whatever life it has.

The first great influence, I suppose if I start "from the beginning," is the Book of Genesis. At the university I won a house debate on the argument that the book was best explained as metaphor and allegory of what nature's Creator did in reality to create reality. So, from the conception, alternative realism, but to a lesser extent also the auto-horrific, are what art is: a metaphor for something inside all of us.

Another influence on my ideas is Shakespeare's *The Tempest*, which in my opinion stands as the most creative drama I have ever seen. The bard's weaving of magic, sorcery, history, and the power of the ideas in Prospero's books, give alternative reality my attempt its ether. The idea stands between reality and fantasy. This is where the auto-horrific, the imagination we all have to create our own reality, even false ones, comes into life.

There are other major artists who give a lot of inspiration. The first is Poe and in particular *The Fall of the House of Usher*. That novella created something so unreal but gave it a horrifying plausibility. The second of these artists is Hesse— everything I ever read by him. The disconnects between sanity and insanity that Hesse presents with seamless efforts of creativity provide a link for my desire to write "weird" fiction. The link is between being sane and not knowing if one is insane. That happens all too frequently with people.

Of course, the paintings of Dali should be a major influence on alternative realism and the auto-horrific. They and he are in a way, but more for the illusion of sight that should be incorporated into the stories, not for the insanity itself. Films also have a character of the vision that should make for an alternatively real existence. My favorite for this influencing effect is Weine's *The Cabinet of Dr. Caligari*.

Yet no theory of some reality being the alternative to the one we have, or a theory about scaring the begeebesses out of one's own self, would ever be complete without the master: Kafka. Let nothing more be said about that genius who created worlds out of proportion or an implausible plot being all too possible like *The Trial*, *The Burrow*, or *Amerika!*

With all of these influences now catalogued, what the heck do I think of about "alternative realism and the auto-horrific?" Again, while not near the masterful abilities of these great artists, I try to give a view in my stories, like those found in this book (though not the free-verse "Along Superior's Northwest Shores," which is anomalous), a slant on the perception of being normal, in a normal world, doing normal things, in a state of normalcy, but within the minds of those who live in that reality where everything has turned out different than it should be. That is the alternative realism. But the entire suite is only complete when the people themselves actually create the things they fear happening the most. By having the realism being the alternative to whatever we expect it to be, by imagining the most horrible things short of being in absolute immorality, actually becoming the situation, well, that is where I get the story. I hope that it is at least more entertaining that way. I hope I tell it well enough or better than anyone else could. Otherwise, why should I even make the attempt to create "in the beginning."

The chief motivation for writing in this "not-a-real-genre" genre is the exploration of fear, the fears we all have, or would have, if reality took the incredible path it could to its conclusion. But I also try to explain that the terminus of the alternative reality is something that we could quite easily have avoided. Todd Wilcox could have avoided his fate if he had never created the cult of the imaginatives. Todd the camper (no story relation to Wilcox) would never have to face his conscience or his ostracism if he had made another choice. So, in short, I like to write about how poor choices people make end up being their undoing by deep, sub-conscious fear.

Alternative realism has the quality to be what we all hope to avoid. The auto-horrific is what we determine for ourselves if we are governed by fear instead of faith. Both are sort of a giving life force, the energy of reality, to those monsters we've created in our imaginations. Both are about being so fascinated by the imaginary demon that we cannot help but think about it, until our own seduction with delusion sells our soul to the darkness. At that point, we end up living the exact opposite of what reality should be. Ideas become reality. Just as in art, so it is in life.

The Imaginatives

The entire day, Fred felt disturbed since the morning class where he thought that he actually talked to people in his head. "Real?" he wondered. "Or not real?" He could not decide. When he arrived home he searched his dad's den closet. He waited till after supper, contemplating the good deed. He felt something about that presence. He felt it. He heard it still sometimes. What an evil force! Insanity?

They lived not in a physical community but connected like many sharing brains, all the parts extended from the central nerve, operating according to the prime impulse. As their psycho-spiritual leader, Todd Wilcox thought that morning, "We rule each other strict as a holy order, and serve the whole knowing that belonging, we no longer find ourselves lost as 'schweep.' "Such a thought he gave them, and many similar, during the meditation time. During that time, each one imagined themselves located in the peacock room of Todd's house. There they heard the Will.

Late in the morning congregation, Fred wandered into the meditation the way the others found it--through a strange accident: Todd's mental aura found Fred. The youngster, a very mature 15-year-old Boy Scout, trained in camping, field-craft, and shooting, and the like, asked the others, "How can so many people fit into such a small mind."

Julie Hayes, #22, the welcome committee chair, replied, "Don't be silly. It is because we will it."

"Then how can I wish my body out of this classroom?"

Debra, Imaginative #35, the assistant to the High Priest for plights and queries, responded to Fred. "You can't have that unless you choose to leave."

"What is your name?" Todd asked, not able to penetrate the newcomer's mind.

"I'm Fred."

"Fred, you will forget your playmates and your classmates. Your mind gives you power and freedom from whatever you don't like. We welcome you into our Nerve where you will no longer feel like the 'schweep.' Here you will learn that the power in yourself is greater than any power in the world. It brought you to us and teaches each the golden rule of our existence."

"What is that?" Fred inquired.

In unison, 94 of the Imaginatives answered in a thought of low toned discord, "Only the mind will go where the body can never follow."

Fred did not show during the afternoon Peacock Room virtual gathering. As the central nerve, Todd asked the others if anyone knew Fred. "I feel we should watch him," he informed the others.

When Todd Wilcox set the evening lesson, the question stimulated the meditative thought, creating reality from nothing, where the unreal can exist. "Think my people," he started, "does a weak mind deserve existence. Shouldn't it die rather than continue a meaningless life where a brain is confined to the flesh?" Thus began the debate which Todd conceived when he first contacted Imaginative #2 several years ago.

Julie Hayes, who owned a fanatical, even lusty, love of her power, offered first a reflecting question: Whether Imaginatives did not exist as a superior, hidden race.

"Yes, yes," some thought.

"A clear truism," cited Willie, #52, the one who possessed more capacity than all the members except Todd.

"Of course!" Debra exclaimed. "The world should exist only for those with enough imagination to see the way past the material limits. The world has others like us whom we need to find.".

"Eventually, we must do so, or the world will fear us, seek us and destroy us," Todd thought through the Nerve. "However, we must formulate our plan. There are 94 of us and if we all exert our imagination, like we experimented, we can control the weak and unimaginative people. We can then set the 'schweep' to slaughtering each other, and use our thoughts to control world leaders. Together, we can save the world for our master race and enslave others to serve us."

"Master High Priest, how many noble and gifted minds are there?" asked Bill.

"A few score thousand, and probably no more."

Todd paused. Echoing a message, he passed the command, fulfilling his dream, the goal toward which he slowly brought along the Imaginatives. "We start now, before anyone can stop us."

Across town, in the fall evening, Fred trudged dressed in his Scout uniform. He spied on the cult because he had superior, though not mature power: he could hide from them. He felt his pocket, then let a sigh once he took a full breath. He stopped in front of the old Victorian house where a psychiatrist lived. Fred stood for long seconds. His palm sweating, his heart churning, he opened the green picket gate that swung on rusty hinges. He approached the mauve door along a crumbling cement walkway. The brown house, its ledges and trimmings painted dark colors of purple, blue, red, and cream brought a cold, wintery shiver to Fred.

Climbing the steps, Fred opened the door. He heard the electric hum coming from the room behind closed doors. Sliding one open, Fred entered the green painted room where peacock printed tapestries hung in the inner-chambered mad-castle of Doom. In the chair sat the brown haired doctor holding in his right hand a bright blue, humming, oval orb.

The doctor opened his spectacled eyes. He looked at the pudgy Fred, his freckled faced covered by a blonde hair lock escaping his hat's brim. The doctor stood, shouting. "Why, you little brat. Who told you could enter in my house? Get out before I call the cops."

Fred slipped from his pocket a snub nosed revolver. He leveled it.

"Fred?" said Dr. Todd Wilcox.

BANG! The bullet slammed hard into Todd's

chest. Fred walked over and pointed the pistol dead range and put another bullet through Todd's ear. A yellowy and reddish gravy squeezed from the other ear. Fred stood above Todd and then Fred turned and aimed straight down at the humming orb on the floor. Two shots. CRACKLE and SPLATTER. So ended the cult of the Imaginatives, for now.

Darkness of the Lake

Todd brought his heavy, bulging pack down to the shoreline of small stones and set the large rucksack in the center of the canoe, just ahead of the broken cross bar.

"Are you sure this will float? I don't think it looks seaworthy," he said.

"Todd, we're a long way from the sea. We're just going across the river," Cameron said approaching the second canoe with his light, smartly organized green pack.

Blake locked the doors to his brand new 4x4 using the button on the key chain. Tightening the straps on his back pack which sat on the open tailgate, he then picked up his gear and slammed the gate shut. Once he put his red rucksack behind the broken cross bar, he said, in disparagement, "This thing is going to buckle on us, Cameron. Why didn't you borrow a non-broken canoe?"

"Will you guys stop being afraid? You'll be fine," Cameron replied, walking back to the shore with the paddles from the bed of Blake's truck, yelling to Jaime, his wife, to be sure to lock the back doors of their old, economy hatchback car.

Within minutes, the four of them pushed off from the landing and paddled the two canoes with heavy and firm strokes to cut across the river's current which was made strong and high because of the dam open far upstream. Blake and the couple each made fluent twists and turns with the paddles, experienced using the feathered J-stroke which caused less resistance in the water and kept the canoe from turning with each stroke. It did not weary the arms as much as Todd's plodding motion which caused drag every time his hand holding the stem of the paddle sloshed into the very clean, almost clear water.

Two hundred yards down the river and traveling across from the starting point, Cameron turned his head behind and yelled, "How is it holding up?"

Todd stopped the monotonous paddling to look behind him. "It's buckling a little!" Resuming, Todd thought about the cold autumn water and shouted, "Hey, why the hell aren't we wearing life jackets."

Cameron shouted that they didn't need them and to "stop being such a chicken."

The 50-degree morning temperature did not chill the overdressed Todd. The sun, beginning to shine through the high hanging fog, warmed the front of this face, cold on the side from the north wind, and the sun shone in his eyes until he pulled the visor of his baseball cap further down over his eyes.

The wide mouth of the slough drew the canoes into its current. Around a spit of land, Cameron and Blake steered the canoes into a depression where the higher than average water ended in a sloppy mess of long, wet grass, mud and brush.

"See, no problem."

"Yeah, yeah," Blake said back to him.

Unloading the equipment, they dragged the canoes over an embankment into another depression higher than the water, and they nestled the canoes behind some bushes and tied them to a small tree.

When everyone had mounted their packs on their backs, Todd adjusted his straps to loosen them over the bulk of his expensive fleece shirt. Cameron called the others to follow him, as he and Blake knew the way. In broad file, they walked up the hill strewn with the outcropping of rock and small wild brush and thorns. The forest of open hardwoods among short, soft, sparse grass held among their tops the sun melted mist of the morning dew. Over fallen logs--some fresh from summer storms, others rotten from the contact with the ground--the group trudged to the top of the ridge and turned to the southeast. At a still, stale, green pond of foul smelling weeds and mud they descended from the ridge toward the sun, keeping the pond to their right. Todd all the while felt the tightness in his fat, out-of-shape thighs and the heavy dampness from his neck down because he overdressed from inexperience and was carrying a pack over broken terrain. Through the trees with brown, orange, yellow, red, gold and even some green leaves, Todd saw the lake's shimmering glare in the small waves made by the breeze.

"Do you see the table?" Cameron asked Blake.

"It should be over there." he replied, scratching his beard. "Todd," he yelled, "You've never been here?"

"No," Todd said, huffing from the back behind the physically fit and blonde Jaime.

"What's that?"

"No!"

When the group arrived within fifty yards of the high edge of the lake, Blake said, pointing to his left, "There it is."

Walking toward the primitive campsite, Cameron said to his wife, "There's Mount Maureen."

"Which is what Todd would like to do."

"Hey, be nice," Todd shot back.

The all-wood picnic table, its lower parts covered in algae and rotting around its feet, had probably floated to the backwater during a flood. Cameron, Blake, and the fun-loving Maureen found it years earlier resting against a tree further down the shore of the backwater lake.

"What a great day." said Cameron, his eyes shaded by the broad brimmed leather bush hat. "I bet there's fish in there," he continued as his eyes scanned the small lake, ringed with lily pads. The occasional ring of rising fish broke the surface.

"Let's set up camp so we can find out," Blake said, slipping out his right shoulder from under the strap of his pack, setting the bag on the table before slipping out the other arm.

"How about Todd and I help each other set up the tents and you two gather firewood," Cameron directed.

Todd and Cameron set up Cameron's small green tent, big enough for two people with an all-encompassing rain fly and a vestibule on the front big enough to store two packs and cook under if it rained. When Todd took out his tent, Cameron asked him, "Going on safari? Let me hold that. Holy s---, it must weigh 12 pounds. I can't believe you actually carried that thing."

"It's not too heavy."

"Where did you get it?"

"Discount store."

It took Todd several minutes to remember how to set up the yellow shelter. The orange rain fly only covered the upper third of the structure.

"You better hope it doesn't rain. You won't be very well protected."

"We'll be fine."

Blake and Jaime gathered a pile of medium thick sticks broken by hand and foot and Blake used a flammable putty to light a small teepee of brush and kindling. White smoke rose and moved with the strengthening breeze. Cameron thought a saw wasn't necessary. It added weight. And he thought a hatchet was just downright dangerous.

"You're using fire starter?" Cameron asked and scoffed. He dug in his pack and pulled out a red bottle of all-purpose gas and a metal tripod underneath a circular burner connected to a hose. Attaching the reinforced rubberized tube to the bottle, Cameron pumped it to pressurize the bottle, then he turned the valve open and used a kitchen match to ignite it. "Time for coffee," he announced.

As they sat around waiting for the white

enameled speckled green coffee pot to perk, the fire in the circle of rocks began to feed, with voracious energy, on the wood set in lean-to fashion as it began to dry from the flame. The smoke of the wet wood grew thicker driving the few late season bugs from the campsite. Some of the wood began to steam and from others tree sap began to bubble out the ends.

Cameron began assembling the five short sections of his fly rod. Attaching the reel, he bent the line above the filament leader and formed a loop on the white floating line. Taking the top of the loop, he threaded the eyes of the rod. Taking out a small box, he patiently examined the contents, lost in thought before selecting and attaching a tiny size 18.

When the coffee had boiled over and Cameron turned down the flame, Blake began to twist the shortened pieces of his collapsible rod, extending the sections and twisting the opposite way to lock them. With a red and white oval-ish metal lure with a trident hook, he went down the steep embankment with high browning grass to the edge of the water. The tall Cameron donned and zipped his light green cotton vest and poured himself a small plastic cup of coffee, adding sugar and powdered cream. Todd poured the coffee into his new stainless steel mug and burned his lip as he tried to sip his black coffee.

With his coffee cup and rod in both hands, Cameron walked to the embankment where it descended less sharply to a small depression with a fallen tree lying crossways back from the lake. He set his coffee on the end of the nearly limbless tree near where the beavers had felled it. Pulling out line and flipping the end of the rod up and down, the fly on the end of the line unfurled. Using a disciplined motion of 10 and 2 o'clock, Cameron used the traditional cast moving the end of the rod gently straight forwards and back, keeping his wrist rigid, creating a loop which crossed under itself in the white floating line as it traveled far ahead and far behind, keeping the fly with its needle sharp hook away from the tall grass. After three or so revolutions, the fly at the end of the tippet settled with ease on the surface of the water before any part of the filament or leader hit the water. Taking in the excess slack, Cameron reached for his coffee and took a drink. To anyone who knew, the cast would be masterful, but to Todd, who looked from the long raised log bench behind the fireplace, it meant nothing.

Looking at the large hill on a half-circle of land extending out on the other side of the lake, Todd's gaze fixated on the landmark called, in affection by the others, Mount Maureen. Taking his camera from the top compartment of his pack, Todd walked to the edge of the embankment, sat on the fat part of a fallen, limbless tree and watched the swarms of ducks passing above. The season began the next morning and Cameron had warned everyone to prepare for loud gunshots and roaming boats early Saturday.

Down below, Blake flung the line heavy with the large lure in an underhand cast far out in the lake. Each time as he reeled in, the hooks brought back the samples of lilies and weeds floating on the surface close to the shore. Cameron continued to watch his line drift in the waves made by the wind, now increasing as the morning passed. Every five to ten minutes, he would retrieve his line to dry cast the water from it and again with gentle motions set the fly on the surface. Todd took a couple of snapshots of the ducks overhead and those landing in the water and shots of Blake and Cameron.

"I got one!" Cameron shouted just as Todd watched him raise the long fly rod to set the hook. Spinning the reel, Cameron pulled in a small mouth bass, large enough for him to measure against the duct taped markings attached at intervals on the long cork handle. "Legal!" he announced.

Putting the bass into a plastic grocery bag once he removed the hook, he used the same casting method to try for another one.

"I'm going a ways to try and find a spot not so weedy," Blake yelled.

A half hour before noon, Todd and Jaime had set out fixings for ham sandwiches and re-ignited the stove to make noodle soup. When the soup boiled to readiness, she shouted to the other two for lunch. The group ate the meal around the campfire which Todd had enthusiastically kept going to ward off the increasing chill of the autumn wind.

"Did you get any bites?" Cameron asked Blake.

"Once I got the hell away from those weeds. It wasn't easy but there's a spot halfway to the beaver lodge where it's not so bad."

"How deep do you think the lake is?" Cameron asked Blake.

"I'd say about four or five feet."

"I thought it would be deeper than that."

"Rice Lake?" Todd added. "Does that mean that wild rice used to grow here?"

"Yeah," Cameron said back to him, "the park guide talks a little about it."

"Are we in the park?" Jaime asked.

"No, we're on public land. I'm not sure if we are even allowed to camp here. Once, after we had been here a couple of times, I called the ranger station and asked. The guy said, 'Who's going to know anyway?' So, I figured that settled the question."

"Where is that beaver lodge?" Todd asked. "I should get a picture of it."

"It's about half way down to the north side of the lake. It's close to the shore."

A large flock of ducks flew down from the northeast across the lake in two large inverted "Vs," one inside of the other.

Cameron commented with wry words as the ducks flew over the campsite, "Those ducks better not crap on us."

"I'll help with the dishes when I get back. I'm going down a ways." Blake said.

"I'll do them," Jaime said.

Far off they heard several resonating and interlocking rumbles of thunder. From the direction of the river westward behind the ridgeline they could see low clouds through the shedding trees.

While the fishermen went in opposite directions along the embankment, Todd sat on the log bench. Pulling a small pair of binoculars from his heavy rubber raincoat pocket, he scanned through the tree line along the water on the far shore to the north of Mount Maureen. It looked like another lake through the branches of a tree line. Curious for a better angle, he stood and walked in the direction of the beaver lodge. With his eyes looking through the binoculars in the disappearing sunlight, he heard a loud slap-splash from below. Walking the edge of the bank, he looked and saw a beaver emerge from below the surface. It traveled in a small circle, its thick hairs streaked back along its body, its face and rump above the water as it swam. Another splash with a long flat tail and it disappeared before Todd returned with his camera. The beaver swam along the shore toward where Cameron fished. Todd followed along and finally snapped a couple of photographs between times when the beaver circled before diving.

A lone brown wood duck landed suddenly close to shore. As the duck came closer to him, Todd took out a facial tissue and broke off pieces to throw as an enticement. Cameron looked over toward the beaver that he followed with his eyes to make sure it didn't get hooked or tangled. As the duck scooped up the bits of tissue with its bill Todd broke off more and the pieces gathered just a foot off the grass shoreline. Todd bent to his knees carefully. The duck came closer; close enough to caress. Todd reached out with more tissue and opened his hand palm upward. The rest of the tissue blew away from a gust of wind. The whole sky had become covered with gray. Thunder came and there fell sprinkles of rain. With a lightning motion Todd swiped at the duck and grabbed it by the neck. The duck's head went limp with a noise like a breaking twig.

"What happened?" Todd asked. "I just wanted to pet it."

"You snapped its neck you dumb-shit." Cameron yelled. He had seen the whole thing from twenty yards away.

Todd opened his grip and the duck fell into the water with a lifeless splash, a loud thud of dead weight. "I didn't mean it."

"You asshole." Cameron said.

"Honestly! I didn't mean to kill it!"

"Well, you should have thought about what might happen!" Cameron yelled. "Why can't you respect anything?" Still upset, he brought in his line and set the hook on the small eye by the cork handle. As Cameron grabbed his empty coffee cup and walked past him, Todd followed him for a couple steps.

"But I didn't know it would happen!" Todd yelled. Jaime walked to the top of the oval depression. She looked down. Blake had heard the commotion and ran because he thought something had gone wrong.

"What do I do now?" Todd asked.

"That's your problem. You better hope a game warden doesn't come here and see it," Cameron said walking up the embankment.

"What's the big deal? It's only a damned dead duck!" Todd shouted.

Jaime folded her arms and walked back to the fire. Blake reached the campsite.

"What happened?" he asked.

Cameron shouted so loud it could be heard on Mount Maureen, "That asshole broke the neck of a duck!"

"Why the hell did he do that?" Blake wanted to know.

"Because he doesn't belong out here," Cameron replied and turned to walk to the campfire.

"It's not my fault! I didn't know it would happen!" Todd shouted, again and again, looking behind him to see the duck drifting out into the lake as the spattering rain sprinkled on the surface of the water. "It's not my fault," Todd repeated. The others had stopped listening.

The Honor of Owning Billy Bill's Bones

Karl wondered who felt more pain, his friend or himself. Billy's breathing came irregular and unmeasured, gasping like children's fits, fighting a horde of dreamy, sleep-time ghosts. Karl held his hand. Billy's crushing clutch pressed Karl's wedding ring, denting it where it met knuckle beside it.

"Karl, Karl," Billy began but started coughing. "Karl, my friend, don't forget what you promised me ten years ago. It's all written down in my will. The lawyers have prepared everything. You will do it, won't you?"

Karl looked at his friend, hearing the respirator pump oxygen through Billy's nostrils. Seeing the tubes reminded Karl that his Aunt Lucy died the same way and looked much the same, though his friend still had hours, perhaps a day before death.

"Yes, Billy," he could not refuse his suffering friend. "I'll do it."

"Exactly as we talked about," coughing again, Billy cleared his throat of phlegm and spit it out into a pan.

"Yes, Billy, exactly as we planned."

"Good, good. That's what a dying man wants to hear. His last wish affirmed. Not much time left, buddy. I'm a goner, maybe tonight. How is Linda going to handle it?"

"Well, she won't have a choice. It was a pact made between you and me a long time ago, before I ever met her."

In a slow sequence, Billy hit the drip and before much time passed he closed his eyes and fell asleep. Karl stood watching his friend's shrunken body heave with the strained, cancered lungs trying to pump air. Then Karl looked at Billy's face: the loose, pale skin dangling from his jowls, the dark set eyes, the skin discolored like a Pharaoh's in colors of blue and purple. Karl let go his hand and left so Billy could sleep.

William Simpson Williams III died about twelve hours later at 4:32 AM. Karl, as arranged, got the call and did what needed doing because Billy had no living relative save a senile, old mother living in the nursing home wing of the same hospital.

The memorial, with no body, took place a few days after the death. Karl eulogized for twenty minutes, highlighting parts of Billy's life. "Although my friend was a humble factory worker, and loved his job, he had a quest of adventure and knowledge which led him on travels around the world, meeting interesting people, and bringing back a compassion for humanity which encouraged him to volunteer to help the needy."

After the service, Tom approached Karl and Linda. "So what's science going to do with Billy's body?"

Karl looked at his wife. "Well," he stammered, "you might as well know as everyone will find out about it later. Billy's vitals and organs were given to science. His body, however, is currently being cleaned."

"What the hell did you do to him?" Tom asked.

Linda's face became very long and her eyes widened.

"It was his dying wish. Next week, his bones will be bathed in acid and bleached."

"Why would he want to do that to himself?" Linda wondered aloud.

"Where's he gonna go?" Tom seemed disbelieving.

"Well," Karl stammered for a brief second, "he wants me to put his high school letter jacket on him, put a can of beer and a cigarette in his hand and stand him up in the corner of our basement so he's there when we party."

"Are you sure that's what he wanted?" Linda demanded to know.

"It sounds like something Billy would want," Tom said, appearing comfortable now that he knew the whole plan. "We'll have to have a party when you set him up. When will that be?"

"The guy taking care of it all said about a couple weeks."

Tom walked away to tell the others. Linda whispered loud and indignant, "There's no way, Karl, that you're bringing Billy's skeleton into my house.   You should have talked to me about it before you agreed to do it."

"I agreed to it three years before we met. And this isn't the place to discuss it.   And there's no discussion. It was his dying wish."

"Uh-uh. No way, absolutely not. I don't care if he was your best friend. We're not doing it."

"We have to," Karl said. "And that's final."

Linda turned her back to him. Walking away, she approached her best friend, Rosa, someone Billy had dated a few years back.

For the next two weeks, Karl and Linda did not discuss the issue. They had no friction during this time, which Karl found odd considering Billy's wish. Karl, as always, slumbered heavily. Not even her usual middle morning bathroom trips disturbed his rest.

At last, on the day of Billy's homecoming, Karl took an afternoon PTO on a very, very hot Wednesday.

"Where do you want it?" the truck driver asked as he pushed the big tall box on a trolley.

"Down in the basement," Karl replied, then helped the man descend the cold concrete steps through the laundry and furnace portion downstairs and into the section decorated in a perpetual festival atmosphere of band posters, beer and liquor signs, and un-lit Christmas lights.

"What's in here anyway, if you don't mind me asking?"

"Billy's bones."

"Who's Billy?"

"My best friend from high school," Karl replied with matter-of-factness and some teasing pleasure.

"You mean I was carrying a dead guy in the

truck?"

"Don't worry, I have all the licenses and permits and stuff."

The deliveryman, in great reluctance, helped Karl remove the top board of the crate with a crowbar, and then they lifted Billy's white skeleton out and hung him on a hook from the rafter near the corner by a chain screwed into Billy's skull.

"If you don't mind, I'll just take the crate and get the hell out of here."

"Right. Thanks for your help."

Karl noticed the time and set Billy's ripped and torn letter jacket on the bar. He shut off the lights, closed the door and ran upstairs. He figured Linda would like the situation better if she did not know until several days passed. That night Karl and Linda watched television after they ate dinner. Ten o'clock came and as usual they went to bed and had sex. Karl's eyes closed and fell comfortably asleep. He dreamt of sitting with a drink in his hand on a beach, smoking a big fatty, having his feet massaged by a Victoria's Secret model wearing nothing save swimming suit bottoms and a seashell necklace.

"Karl," he heard the model say, "wake up! Somebody's in the house!"

"Oh, don't worry baby, there's nobody here but you, me, sand, and ocean."

"Karl, wake up!" he heard again. Coming conscious, he felt a hand shake his shoulder.

"Karl," Linda whispered loud though trying to keep quiet, "somebody's in the house!"

"Wha?" he said, sitting erect, tuned and listening.

Telling Linda to stay quiet and lock the door, in the hallway he heard the lock click. He could hear the creaking noise better, a sound which the old house made when someone walked the floors. He reached the living room entrance, seeing the kitchen sink light that illuminated both rooms. No one lurked here. He checked around: door locked tight, windows secure. When he reached the kitchen, he checked the back door and realized, horrified, that the sound originated downstairs.

Karl summoned courage. Very freaked, he grabbed the railing. With slow, reluctant movements, he stepped down the concrete steps that seemed like they oozed unusual cold and dampness. He turned the doorknob. Across the room, behind the furnace that blocked most of the view, he saw the brightness that the Christmas lights made--greens, reds, oranges, yellows, and blues. "Did I leave the lights on?" he wondered. Swallowing his own heart, he freed himself from the choking sensation that swelled over his trembling body. Now, he could hear the loud, steady, rhythmic creaking.

"HOLY SHIT!" he said, then repeated thinking, nay pleading, "Oh, Jesus, oh, Jesus, oh, Jesus. I promise I'll never get stoned again. I'll never get stoned again. Just don't let it be Billy. Don't let it be Billy."

Past the washer, the dryer and the tub he moved, trepidly. Around the sleeping furnace, and just as he made his last step, Karl closed his eyes, saying one more time, "I'll never smoke pot again."

He opened his eyes. In the corner, swinging in the central air breeze blowing from an open vent, he saw Billy Bill's bones. The creaking, rubbing chain jostled Karl's hearing as he experienced shocking delirium. Billy's skull and leg bones glistened and shone the varied colors of the lights reflecting on white. Karl's mouth fell open, standing there, unmovable. His skin turned sick, pale. There swayed his best friend in his green letter jacket with the white leather arm of his right sleeve pinned to his chest, holding a beer can. A cigarette jammed in the mouth's corner jutted out from the sinister, smiling golden teeth.

Karl found movement, running upstairs, closing the basement door as he passed. He hit the central air dial in the living room. The creaking ceased seconds later. Shaking with cold pellets of sweat, he pounded the bedroom door.

"It's me. Open up. Everything's okay."

Linda unlocked the door. "What was it?"

"Oh, I must have left a vent open in the basement earlier. The air just bounced my spiced rum mirror off the wall."

"Why are you sweating?"

"Well, I just got pretty nervous until I found out what it was," he said. "Let's just go back to sleep."

Once Linda dozed, breathing relieved and relaxed, Karl locked the door. His heart beat fast all night.

Morning came. He kissed Linda good-bye as she left. Walking into the basement, still suffering the fast beating anxiety and chokiness, he entered the Christmas lighted part. Billy still looked evil to him, even though morning light shone through the small window. Carrying the bones to his car trunk, he sped away, using the rear-view mirror to watch the backseat. He stopped by to see Tom, who had just arrived home after his swing shift.

They exchanged small talk, and then Karl said, "You know, Tom, Linda doesn't want Billy's bones in the house. I have to respect her wishes or I might never get laid again. Why don't you take them? You don't have anyone living with you."

"Sure." Tom told Karl. "It would be an honor to keep Billy Bill's bones."

All day while working, the slightest sound in the hardware store made Karl jump. He told himself that he would break his rule and smoke a joynt during the week when he made it home. When he entered the house, Linda was putting groceries away.

"Hey, when do those damned bones get here?"

"Oh, yeah, I decided that since it really bothered you so much and freaked you out, I asked Tom if he would take them. They should have been delivered today."

"Why, thank you, sweety, that's real considerate of you."

"Yeah, it's asking a lot from you. Anyway, I'm going to go down and burn one."

"On a weekday?"

"Well, why not? In honor of Billy."

"I'll be down when I finish the groceries."

Karl disappeared to the basement. After a couple minutes, Linda picked up the portable phone and dialed Rosa, her best friend.

"Hey, it's me. I just thought I would call and say that it worked. That was a great idea. Remember, don't tell anyone. Call me later."

Setting the phone on the counter and smiling, she walked to the basement stairs.

The Evil of the Sub-Demon

"There's a bunch of noise outside my room," he told the man on the phone. "The sirens, voices, screaming, and shouting. Tell them to please stop it. I can't handle it. It's driving me batty."

The night manager said he would investigate.

"Thank you," Brad said, turning his body to replace the receiver.

When his arm reached the nightstand it lost its strength as it limped and rested on the fake wood. His head burrowed the pillow and he sat breathing the carbon dioxide. When he picked up his head, the wetness remained on the pillow. At once, though, the sweat built on his forehead and moisture further dampened his already greasy black-dyed hair.

With assembled strength, he drank some ice water. Holding the glass to his brow, the coolness removed some of the heat swirling in his body. Outside, he could hear the voices. The sirens bellowed, sounding just feet away from his first level window.

"Good Lord," he said.

Inside him, the thought roved and occupied his thinking, disjointed like an amputee from his severed forearm, wanting something unknown, unattainable, and altogether not what he presently had. Like allergic muscle and skin, his whole body experienced the unstoppable twitch. His sinew and tendons ripped crunchy noises like taut rope, twisting, stretching. Every cell in him seemed to split apart, leaving an opening that only a fix could fill and restore.

The phone rang.

"Hello," Brad said with wet, dribbling saliva escaping from the lip's corner.

"Yes, sir, this is the night manager. I just went outside and I didn't see anything."

"Did you hear it at least?"

"No, sir, I heard nothing. Everything is peaceful outside."

"That's impossible. I can hear it now. They're right outside."

"What do you see outside your window, sir?"

"I can't see. I have my curtains drawn."

"Take a look, sir," the manager instructed.

"I'll look in a minute. I have to use the bathroom."

Brad replaced the phone. Resting on his back, he examined the ceiling. A shivering shook his body and continued to the ends of his arms, continuing unceasing patterns. Sitting erect, he put his feet on the floor, stomping them. Remaining still further maddened the shiver.

One more time looking through his brown canvas duffel bag, he found nothing of use. An empty sandwich bag licked clean, and clean and useless tools: a spoon and a needle. Standing, his legs encountered nervy roadblocks of gummy residue. The knees bent, the body fell, collapsing him and doubling him, as he held his stomach like he got sucker punched. Crawling, the trip took slow-motioned minutes, creeping interrupted where he convulsed. Then he puked, leaving the toilet water a greenish fluid the color and consistency of a mint milkshake. Brad washed his face from the bathtub faucet, dowsing his hair as he held his head beneath the cold stream. Holding a long time, the frigid rivulets flowed on his neck, soothing the temperature, now a bearable, brief simmer relieving the inner friction. Walking out of the bathroom, Brad rubbed the scabby, infected sores on his left arm, all dried blood the color of brown gargoyle skin, or so he used to joke in more care-free times.

Summoning vigor, Brad stood and walking a woozy stumble to the bed, he continued hearing the sounds. "Hey, Brad," he heard. It sounded like Scuzzi-John. "Hey, Brad, you okay? Do you need more?"

With eyes closed Brad yelled, "Yeah, I need more. I need more right now. How much?"

"It's on the house. Just call room service."

Brad opened his eyes, though they remained hair thin slits and dialed the phone.

"Front desk," the man said.

"I would like to order room service. John told me you could help me."

"Room number?"

"129."

"Oh, jeez," Brad heard him say. "How can I help you, sir?"

"I would like some speed please. And if you could, send me a rock and I really, really need some dope."

"Pardon me, sir, but we don't have that. I can't help you."

"But Johnny said. . ."

"Sir, excuse me, I have to register someone."

"But Johnny . . . ." Then silence.

"JOHNNY!" The loud shout reverberated Brad's incomprehensible world.

A knock.

"Brad, it's your cousin. Open the door."

"Marcy," he said when he lifted his head. "Marcy, it can't be you."

"Brad, it's me. Let me in."

"Marcy, you're dead."

"No, I'm not dead. I'm alive and I want to help you. Open the door." Brad heard pounding.

"Marcy!" He kneeled on the yellow bedspread and stepped forward falling, stumbling as his head hit the heavy door. "Marcy!" He opened and looked, seeing a woman, older and dressed in a black polyester ladies suit, walking past with a bucket full of ice. Putting his head into the hall he looked both ways.

"Marcy," he whispered.

The woman, who passed him, tried not looking. Stepping straight back, Brad leaned forward against the closed door. "Oh, Marcy, why did you have to die?"

"I didn't die, Cousin. I'm right here."

Turning around, there she stood--white prom

dress, curled hair high and bow tied. The plush red rose corsage on her chest billowed, exploded.

"Marcy." He spoke her name, relieved.

"Brad, I've come to say I'm sorry."

"Sorry?"

"I wish I had never gotten you high for the first time. But that's what happened. You have lived a very hard life, Cousin. No matter what, you had to live through everything just to get where you will go from here. We are watching you, keeping you near us. You need never fear. He is always with you."

"Who? Who is always with me? Who are 'we'?"

"You are almost done with the hard part. Hold on. It will begin to get better very soon. Ask him and you will receive peace."

Standing there, his drooping jaw opened, exposing yellow teeth, Brad could no longer hear the commotion. Neither could he speak.

"I must go now. I love you, Cousin. I'm always with you. He is always with you. We are always with you."

She turned, walking away. He followed her, struggling though keeping upright. Reaching the bathroom door, he turned and looked. He saw an empty room.

"Marcy," he whimpered, still looking into the shower.

"Brad! Hey, Brad! Can I come in!"

"Johnny! Where are you?" Brad spun to move toward the bed.

"I'm right here," John said. Five inches from his face, Brad stood before the death and misery dealer. The peddler's brown beard and dread locks, even his eyebrows, fell mangled and unwashed. He smiled at Brad, revealing the three remaining brown and black teeth.

"Want some, man?"

John held a black metal syringe. It had a glass vial exposed between the needle and plunger.

Brad began salivating so that clear, bubbling fluid dripped down his chin's crease. Reaching, using a hesitant gesture, he then yanked back his hand. "No."

"No? Come on Brad, you know you want it. You need it. You can't live without it."

"No," Brad repeated. He fell past Johnny landing on the bed, sliding to his knees. Clasping his hands, he stretched them forward. "NO, NO, NO, NO. PLEASE, PLEASE, PLEASE!"

Knock, knock, knock.

"Mr. Kalna? Mr. Kalna? Are you okay? This is the sheriff's department. We would like to talk with you a minute. Your mother is with us and she is worried about you. Please open up."

Then John told his most often willing victim, "If you don't want it, Bradley, maybe your mother does!"

"NOOOO!" Brad yelled loud as a rumbling tornado. Jumping, Brad tackled Johnny. "NO! NO!" Brad grabbed the syringe. Holding it high, Brad thrust it downward.

A loud thundering, fierce Satanic painful sound bounced. The dealer's head tore apart through the skin and muscle, uncovering brown leather, old, abused suede holding big round black eyes, a square nose, and black-fanged mouth. Red corpuscles ran throughout the face. The demon struggled as he burst free from the old ripped and frayed denim clothes, showing his lanky, bony frame and giant wings connected by sinews like black spider webs.

Brad continued stabbing as thick, brown devil's blood splew across his face and shirt.

The door opened. The night manager stepped aside leaving the card key in the slide, allowing two deputies poised with pistols to plant themselves. Brad stabbed as brown strings rose every time he raised his arm, twisting them around his hands.

The police officers replaced their pistols, then jumped on Brad, and held him. "Get the syringe," one said to the other.

"Brad, oh, Brad," his mother wept entering the room behind the night manager.

"Calm down, son, calm down," One deputy said, as they both restrained him. "You killed it. You killed the bag."

Brad stopped resisting. He looked over to his left. On the floor of the bathroom he saw a brilliant red rose corsage.

Along Superior's Northwest Shore

Along Superior's northwest shore, the challenge
of walking invites us.

The first step on the dirt path, or up the rock
steps,

or along the corduroy logs over musty smelling
mud, frees me.

I can't see through the side of a thick grove of
pine

in which a tunnel points straight through to the
light

on the other side of the morning's lower mist.

The water of recent rain–it always seem to rain–
lies in slog

and the puddle seeps through my boots,

never proof enough against the stepping on the
early dew.

My socks soak and introduce my feet to toil.

On the trail I have traveled–five or six miles on a day
Up along the bluffs, hoping to catch a whiff of air on a scorching,
wet summer afternoon, so windless that the great lake looks solid-smooth
and steams off water in a haze through which I cannot see.
Or I walk along a cliff free of trees and I can see the marsh below
surrounded by pines and ash, filled with pads and lodges
Made by nature's great engineer on top of whose dams over laid with boards
I cross streams filled on one side into a pond.

I journey for days with a bag of home on my back, a climb straight up the Drain Pipe
or Wolf's Rock to camp at Palisade Creek or Gooseberry run
or Split Rock flow, or in passing the power of nature
thundering over Baptism's Falls.
I walk on web shoes in snow on the switchback sides of Leveraux on a clear
blue day in winter and ascend Trudee above clouds that sweat.

I see the startled deer.
I cross the bear paw print in spring goo.
I hear the flutter and briefly see the alarmed wings of grouse.
I touch the yellow leaves of an autumn turning

maple.

I smell the pollen of a thousand cattails.

I see the green carpet of blades of grass among the nettled statues

  atop Christmas Tree Ridge.

I hear the trickle and trackle as the stream beneath the covered footbridge

  runs into the miner's shaft.

Through the leaf-less birch frosts of morning I see the big lake miles away from my hill.

When done walking I lay down my bronze-headed cane.

I feel the tight and sore of my calves and thighs, the rest of easy breathing,

  the ache of my shoulder under the rubbing and chafing of a strap relieved.

My friend and I pitch our tent in the woods.

We boil and perk our kettle of ashened coffee on a fire whose sticks we have gathered

  and snapped with our hands.

We cook our salty noodles or plain rice or spuds on a stove, garnishing with bread,

  dried, tangy venison, sweet water-free fruit, nuts, and chocolate.

Sitting there, with my shoes removed and my socks airing, I read Thucydides

  on the ground or sitting on a carved out bench.

I serenely hear and see and smell and taste and touch-- thoughtlessly feel the place around me.

I write in my orange bound journal–"I've come back to the woods. This IS living!"

Quixote of River City

Watching his television, connected to a video tape player, Brad Kalna heard the words, YOU CAN DO THAT. The words emanated not from the illegal copy of the movie. Neither of the Brother Friars on the screen had uttered them; nor did a narrator relate them. The words came from a personal narrator, a distinct voice of command. Brad could hear the words clearly as if someone talked directly into his ear. He always hoped that someone, anyone, would talk to him.

Chairman Meow sat on the rocking chair in the corner of the room and he did not hear the words or they would have startled him. The words repeated, YOU CAN DO THAT. The anonymous spirit dominated Brad Kalna's thoughts. YOU MUST DO THAT. The voice concluded: BECOME A BROTHER FRIAR OF THE WAY

A tear formed in Brad's left eye. It broke free from the lash and streaked down his cheek as another swelled. "I shall be redeemed," he whispered to himself, causing Chairman Meow to lift his head from the chair's seat and look at his Papa.

YOU SHALL BE REVEALED WHEN IT BECOMES REVEALED TO YOU, the form-less voice said.

"I shall be revealed," Brad repeated.

YOU SHALL BE SAVED.

"I shall be saved!" Brad exclaimed, smiling as he rested his head back on the sofa.

Brad straightened his back, leaned forward and repeated to himself, "I must become a Brother Friar of the Way," and again he repeated it. He reached over to the end table and picked up a brass pipe. He put the short stem to his lips and flicked a lighter, touching the flame to the bowl. The dry grass burned and crackled as it glowed a deep orange, turning itself to ash when Brad stopped sucking. Holding his air until it burst forth in a rolling stream of smoke, he coughed and lunged forward with heaves of hammering air. The rush came to his head. It felt like freedom and he closed his eyes. He thought "salvation."

The proxy of self-will said a single word into Brad's ear. HERO. Brad watched the movie until the end where the Friars defeated the conspirator, performing their duty to the Way of order and the balance to the power. Count Moch, the wicked, vile man, defeated; Terrafora saved!

"Oh, the glory," Brad smiled, taking another narcotic pill and a decongestant, washing both down with a swig of cheap brandy. "Oh, glory," he said, gagging from the liquor.

Having stayed up all night, Brad took extra doses of his anti-psychotic and anti-depressant meds. Mid-morning, he walked several blocks. Brad knocked on the door of the house with peeling white paint, a falling porch, and garbage in the yard. The bearded man who answered said, "Hi, Brad. Come on in."

The Dopeman's house had black drapes over the windows, mimicking night. The posters and psychedelic graffiti cards on the walls and ceiling glowered in the red lamps placed throughout the "dead"-room.

Brad sat on the green couch where troll's hair of white stuffing broke through the embroidered fabric.

"How's it going today?" the Dopeman asked.

"Not bad, not too bad at all," Brad said as he straightened out the long-sleeve of his blue shirt. Looking up, he asked, "Got any zoomers?"

"You must be psychic," said the Dopeman. "I just got some and I've got an eighth left."

"How much?" Brad asked. He pulled a fold of cash from his front pocket.

"Fifteen bucks a gram."

"Kind of pricey, isn't it?" Brad commented.

Offended, the Dopeman shot back, "Well, they're a hot item. I'm in business." He paused. "It is the law of supply and demand. I'll cut you a deal though: three and a half grams for fifty bucks."

"I'll take that," Brad said, handing the Dopeman two twenties and ten ones.

"Where do you get all your money?" the Dopeman wanted to know, putting the caps and stems of freeze dried mushrooms into a baggie.

"Why do you care?" Brad asked.

"Just being nosey. I don't really care. You're one of my best customers as long as you got cash."

"I'm independently wealthy," Brad said.

"Good for you," the Dopeman said. He put the bills into a cigar box on the coffee table with other wads of money.

Brad shook Dopeman's hand and left.

Walking home in his brown shoes, Brad passed a lady sitting on the corner bench, resting on her walk up the hill from downtown to the same building where Brad rented his subsidized apartment. The old lady had seen Brad often in and out of the building but had never spoken to him. Brad said a friendly, "Hello." The woman did not respond. Instead, she turned her head away and feigned not hearing Brad. The sadness of the rebuke made Brad think once again, "Why is everyone afraid of me?"

Walking into his apartment full of shelved books coexisting with dishes spilling from the sink to the counter, Brad greeted his cat. "How do, Mr. Chairman?" he said. The cat meowed a welcome and purred when Brad stood by the small table on which the cat sat. The Chairman meowed some more and rolled and purred around while Brad massaged C.M.

From the hiding place behind his set of Edgar Allan Poe, Brad brought out the brass and wood box. He removed the pot pipe and sat on the couch, lighting and sucking. In the relief zone, he closed his eyes and lay down on the sofa with his head on a pillow. He napped for three hours.

In the early hours of that late summer evening, the air got cooler. Brad sat in the breeze that pushed through the window. The slight wind made the see-through curtains blow and sway in rolls of fine, transparent, orangish waves. The light of the blue lamp on the end table illuminated the inside of the apartment as the twilight began to fade into dark before the moon appeared.

The mushrooms–all of them–that he had gagged down with canned spaghetti sauce, had started to work their fungal magic. The gimping started with tightness in his jaw with a metallic taste. At the same moments the stiffness in his neck caused a convulsion beneath his skin. Excess saliva built on the surface of his tongue. A tickle started on the center of his back like a feather brushing the inside of his spine. Brad called that tickle the "unscratchable itch." No amount of rubbing or mind power could make that sensation end while the poison of the mushrooms affected the fluid in his nervous synapses. Brad should have known that only humans among all animals would consciously eat poison.

Hysteria started: The sound of one man tripping as the apartment filled with devious chuckling. Brad's head twirled on his stiff neck and he kept his eyes closed when the waves of heat and cold started in his fingers and toes then swept toward his head. The cold rays of the blue light froze the depth of the room. The old globe, the toy soldiers, the model airplanes, and the prints of Impressionist paintings on the walls... all existed in a space time continuum of unbalanced alignment. The pictures swirled in a melted and moving wax of color–blue, orange, red, yellow and green. The ink on the starry scene and the lilies slithered into endless rivers of slow, self-perpetual deluded, color-laden movement like a river flowing uphill back into itself. The whole room moved in a slow gel like cold time; motion suffered hypothermia in action and it all came back to the beginning, again.

After, the cycle of laughing ended and then came remorse. Like fever and chill, the emotion in Brad alternated with weighted heart, the force of over-thought and feelings rising and falling, changing, growing but going in reverse gravity to thoughts beginning. Every several seconds, Brad switched from the warm then to the self-consciousness of "wrong."

While the stringy-time-controlled flow of color of the pictures moved into rivers of visual ecstasy and wonder, Brad said, "God, why have you forgotten me?"

The appeal to God sounded almost lyrical in the highs and flats of the flutes, the woods, the horns and the strings playing on the stereo. Brad started crying, confused by the beauty of the image, the tone of the experience and the gut-aching self-awareness.

I HAVE NOT FORGOTTEN YOU, the non-spirit voice whispered.

"How do I make friends? How can I make people not fear me?"

FOLLOW THE WAY OF THE BROTHERHOOD AND OTHERS WILL LOVE YOU IN GRATITUDE, the voice said.

"The Way?" Brad said aloud, interrupting the snivel of tears. "Follow the Way!" he said again, louder and hopeful.

FOLLOW THE WAY, the voiced echoed within the cavern of his empty mind.

The cave holding the perception swallowed all

reason and rationality. The voice had ceased. It would come again.

Coming down from the flows and motion of the mushroom trip, Brad sang in quiet, "On a distant shore, miles from land, stands the ebony totem on ebony sand; a dream in a mist of gray."

Not able to move and unwilling to think because thinking hurt the very hair on his head, Brad let meditation overwhelm him like a wave—calm and relaxing. The knowledge filled in him the images and words in block letters envisioned. Brad resolved to become a superman and receive empowerment.

Waking from a sleepless nap, a mere hour before sunrise, Brad stood up from the sofa and he stretched his arms. He could now at last soothe that unitchable scratch. He then slept heavily in his bed for the rest of the day, awaking past sunset, wondering if the daylight passed or if he had awakened within the same night.

"I had better get busy," he said, sitting in the blue lighted darkness of the September evening. "I have to learn the Way."

The next day, Brad visited the public library in the old theater. He borrowed a paperback novel from *The Adventures*, and he brought it home to read. He read all three hundred and fifty pages by late the next morning and played and replayed the movie. The book described the Brotherhood's secrets, the mystical and spiritual principles gained from prayer and meditation.

Upon finishing the paperback, Brad juggled three half-full bottles to the bathroom. Holding the latter bottle, he undid the cap and looked inside. The long, thin yellow capsules plittered when he turned the bottle above the toilet. They made small-circled wakes. He likewise poured the other two bottles into the toilet. Ninety-odd pills of yellow, blue, and purplish-pink. Looking with a feeling of expectant fear, yet feeling willful, Brad pushed the handle and Swoosh! They had disappeared to poison some other sewer rat.

Already a few days without the medication, Brad jumped, jerked, and twitched without control. His sudden and nervous jitter brought him to the bedroom closet. Opening the closet door, he ran his hand over many shirts and pants, bought by his mother. He pulled black woolen trousers from its hanger and flipped them onto the bed. He brushed the shoulders of several shirts, all finely made designer editions. Choosing one off-white turtleneck, he tossed it next to the slacks. He found a black mole-hair sweater. Last, he selected a pair of black wing tips from the closet floor.

Standing, Brand jumped and twitched, at the mirror hanging on the bathroom door. Next to him, looking at Brad's reflection as well as his own, Chairman Meow sat, his black head held high. He meowed no warning. Brad stood wearing his underwear and T-shirt. After a minute, Brad gazed at his fully attired version of the Friar's uniform.

Brad strode back to the closet, fingering the long wooden pole from which dangled the numerous hangers. With tremulous urgency he grabbed armfuls of clothes and dumped them on the floor. Lifting the pole from the slots in the walls Brad grabbed the pole as if he held a Friar's sword. Before the mirror he practiced offense and defense: thrust, parry, jab, slash. The three and a half foot-long, wood stick whipped around as Brad twirled it.

He dropped the "sword" several times. Brad put one hand on the end and whisked it back behind his head, jutting forth the opposite leg, leaning and crouching, the mirror reflecting him. He pulled the "sword" around his body and whipped it up and forward, clasping the "sword" tight with both hands. Lifting his arms high and back...Spratch! The tip of the stick stuck into the overhead lamp's glass shade. The pieces shattered and sprinkled like thick, opaque white snowflakes on the bed and the mauve carpeting.

The phone rang.

"Bradley," the woman's voice said.

"Hello, Mother."

"How are you?"

"I'm fine."

"What have you been doing?" she asked.

"Nothing. I'm just sitting around."

"You sound tired, or depressed."

"I'm just tired. I haven't slept well lately."

"Are you taking your medication?" she inquired.

"Oh, yeah," he lied. "I have just been having bad dreams."

"Those again?" she said. "Perhaps you can ask your doctor next week for a sleeping aid."

"Nah, I'll be fine," he told her.

"Did you want me to come up to go with you to the doctor?"

"No, I'll walk over there myself," he said, beginning to shift on his feet as he stood next to the kitchen counter. He gripped the wooden "sword" tighter with his left hand.

"Well, don't forget to go. You need to keep that up in order to keep getting your SSI." She referred to Supplementary Security Income, a government program that Brad received because of his mental illness. "Do you have any money left this month?"

"I could use a few bucks," he said to her as he sat on the tiled floor so he did not jump on his toes.

"Your father's got a job for you at the plant if you want to move down here and live with us."

"No, I like living here," Brad said. "Did Dad say anything about the money you gave me last month?"

"He knows nothing about it and what he doesn't know won't hurt anything, so don't say anything. Okay?"

"All right."

"May be you should do something today. Get out of the house, call someone to go have coffee with or to see a movie."

"I don't have any friends, Mother! Stop badgering me."

"Sorry. I just thought if you tried to make friends you'll have someone to call so you're not so lonely," she said. "At least go for a walk. Exercise is supposed to help your condition."

"I'm going, now," Brad said standing again. "Good-bye, Mother."

"Wait!" she yelled over the phone. "Wa..." Brad hung up the receiver.

Brad shuttled in short fast steps back to the bedroom a few feet away. "Make friends?" he muttered with disgust. He clasped the "sword" in his hands and stood once again in front of the mirror. When he shuffled his right foot back, he could hear and feel glass flakes crunch under his shoe.

"People don't want to be friends with me!" he shouted lifting the "sword" high above his head. The tip scraped the ceiling and left a brownish mark on the rough surface. With fury he swung the "sword" down and the tip landed on his reflected face. Crash! The mirror split in three large pieces. The two on the bottom and top left stayed in their pegs. The third piece shattered, creating small knives of back-plated glass strewn on the shag carpeting.

A Friar protects the order and balance of power. Only after long years studying, meditating and serving does a Friar enter the higher echelons of the Brotherhood. Experience, Brad reasoned, would come. He could no longer wait.

Brad packed a pipe bowl with the last pot shreds, the shake of his weed. When the flame of the lighter touched the very dry grass, the rushing air and the pop of burning echoed. In the middle of the living room floor he sat crossed-legged. The "sword" sat with one end on the rug, across his body, with the top end resting on the opposite shoulder.

"Oh, Way of the Brotherhood of Friars, guide me toward knowledge and give me wisdom of the world. Oh, mighty Way, reveal to me your secrets," he chanted.

In the silence, the daylight filtered through the open curtains. Brad saw visions. A structure of steel and rock rose skyward. He could also see through the clouds the swirling dark mass of Count Moch, Terrafora's enemy of peace and order, the Brotherhood's foe, the man who challenged the Way. Brad felt the Way inside him, beginning with his fingers and toes, up through his arms and legs, into his stomach and breast, and then finally to his head. The Way of Glory! The Way of Freedom! He had a calm and assured feeling. The Way came to him swelling a cool wave, rushing through the heat of the body; continuous waves; the rippling motion . . . love. Brad's legs twitched and his lips smacked, the quirks of the passing medicine leaving him. At that moment, Brad knew. He had the Way. He had freed himself of the "poisonous" chemicals. He felt the natural power, the Way's power.

Brad stood, letting the "sword" drag on the rug and the tile as he walked to the small kitchen. He found in the drawer a piece of heavy string, long and thick. Brad draped it over his left shoulder so that the two ends hung evenly, front and back. Struggling to keep the calmness and nimbleness so he could do it, Brad tied the front end of the string around the "sword hilt." He grabbed the back string under his arm and jerked down so that the stick slid into his armpit. Brad tied a bow to the wood so that it would come down when he tugged. Opening the closet, Brad removed a fleece insulated, black trench coat that came almost to his ankles. He draped it through his arms and made sure the "sword" did not protrude from the bottom.

In the corner of the mirror, an almost string theory blur of flash-back-like-whizzing-dark atoms appeared in the window behind him. The loud "thump!" caused the hiding Chairman Meow to jump onto the window ledge. Brad turned and stood still. He scooted to the window and looked outside to see a nuthatch, the color of grayish chestnut, on the ground and not moving. Brad ran into the hallway of his building, the door closing and locking behind him, and he ran out the side door, almost tripping over the long stick beneath his coat. Around the corner he found the bird still motionless on the sun-fried grass. Brad knelt by pulling the "sword" behind him and he picked up the bird, resting it in his left palm. He brushed downward the soft feathers using an index finger, massaging the little bird. Still stunned, the bird came awake. It shrugged its head and shivered its wings while perching itself upright on Brad's hand. The bird flapped in fury and flew into a small sapling tree.

YOU HAVE GOT THE GIFT OF LIFE, he heard the voice say. YOU HAVE DISCOVERED THE WAY BEYOND THE WAY.

Brad remained on one knee, expressionless– wide eyed and silent while the voice spoke to him. His uncombed hair, lightened from the summer-time sun, and the thick reddish stubble on his face, created the disoriented appearance. The old woman neighbor looked at him from the sidewalk before entering the building.

BE WARY. MOCH IS WATCHING. Brad began feeling sick, his empty stomach upset not having eaten in two days. He stood and stumbled to the small tree and began at first gagging and then puking clearish liquid at the base of the tree. After heaving several minutes, Brad wiped his mouth with his arm. Sweat began building inside the layers of clothing. Looking up, he noticed the bright equinox sun beating a hard 88 degrees. Walking back to his apartment, he sauntered down the hall and grabbed the doorknob. He twisted and shook the knob. With the backside of his closed fist he gave the heavy wood door a single heavy pound.

"Fuck!" he yelled and the echo bounced between the bare white walls and tile flooring in the hallway.

"Shit," he said.

Outside, he aimlessly wandered in mid-afternoon heat along the hillside sidewalks and streets. After an hour walking, Brad had a thick, salty sweat all over his body. On the same street as his apartment, though two blocks down, he saw a girl turn the corner. She crossed the street toward him and Brad slowed and stared at her as she passed. The brown haired heavy girl gave him a forced, thick-lipped smile. Brad stopped and turned around. He followed her at a distance. Suspicious, the woman turned her head around and noticed him behind her. She waddled faster. She could hear the increased rhythm as Brad's paces quickened. Frightened, the girl ran.

"Wait!" Brad yelled. "Don't be scared! I just want to talk to you! I just want someone to talk with me. Please!"

The woman ran up a cement walkway to a green house and knocked on the door. Brad stood near the street, looking. A man answered the door. Both entered the house, closing the door, while Brad paced on the sidewalk. The man opened the door again and shouted, "If you've got something to say, why don't you come up here and say it!"

Brad shook his head and walked toward his apartment. When he got there he kept walking on the road that followed the contour of the hill. Overhead, black clouds moved fast with the east blowing wind.

At the front door of the broken house, the

Dopeman said, "Hey, Brad." He saw Brad in his heavy clothes, and sweaty, messy hair. Brad's eyes stared past the Dopeman, blank and vacant. "You look like hell," the Dopeman continued.

"Can I come in?" Brad asked.

"Well, I was just going to leave for a little while," the Dopeman lied.

"Please. I'm really hurting."

"Brad, man, you need some help," the drug dealer said rubbing his short black beard. "What do you want?"

"Just a joint."

"You got money?"

"I've got it!"

"Well, come on," the Dopeman said, inviting him into the dark lair. "Just be quick about it."

In the "dead"-room of red light, Brad paced in front of the television showing classic sitcoms. The Dopeman sat down on his couch and rolled a thin joint with the twist of his fat fingers. Licking the glue, the Dopeman closed the paisley papers into a tube. He handed the "pinner" to Brad.

"Can I smoke it here?" Brad asked.

"Aren't you forgetting something?" the Dopeman returned.

Brad dug into his front pants pocket where he had a small fold of a fiver and three ones. "Five bucks okay?" he asked the Dopeman.

"How much you got?"

"Not enough if I'm going to eat anything," Brad said.

"You need to get a job," the Dopeman said while thrusting forward his hand. Brad put the worn Lincoln into the Dopeman's angry grasp.

"Can I smoke it here?" Brad asked.

"I said I've gotta go," the Dopeman said.

"Come on, I locked myself out of my apartment and the super won't be home from his day job til later!" Brad pleaded.

"Make it quick," the Dopeman said.

Brad pulled out a lighter from his pocket and pushed down on the igniter. The flame gave a warm glow to the dark room. Brad touched the flame to the joint that hung loosely from his mouth. Holding the joint with his thumb and forefinger, he sucked the smoke directly into his lungs. The paper and the pot burnt in a dry, crispy fry. Closing his eyes, Brad pulled the joint from his lips, ripping a piece of rolling paper that stuck to his lower lip. He held the smoke for as long as he could, then blew the vapor out with coughs. After several more tugs while still standing in front of the television, Brad snuffed the roach with his thumb on the corner of the ashtray. Brad put the remains into his coin pocket under the belt line of his wool slacks.

"That feels a lot better," Brad said to the Dopeman.

"Yeah, well, I gotta go," the drug dealer said.

Brad exited the door that the Dopeman held open. Without either saying a word, Brad walked onto the broken porch. Behind him he heard the door slam and the lock click. Smiling, Brad walked to the sidewalk, not knowing where he could go but not really thinking about it anyway. His eyes, bloodshot around the dilated pupils, gleamed and dried.

The wind blew leaf fragments, grass cuttings, and road dust. Overhead, a full sky of fast moving black and gray clouds crossed the river, echoing thunder minutes later as the temperature cooled 25 degrees. The rain began in driblets, making wet spotting dots on the cement and blacktop. When Brad reached the next corner a sharp and quick "CRACK!" of close thunder and a bright lightning flash ignited the sky. The raindrops fell fatter and faster. As Brad's greasy bare head began to rinse with the soft, pure rainwater, he began walking down the hill along the street whose gullied sides ran small rivers.

Reaching Main Street, Brad drifted toward the highway walking the muddy path that began past the fire station. As he moved beyond the business district the cars and trucks with their headlights glowing threw water with their tires. He walked among the taller trees and thick bushes following another winding trail that led toward the river. Not moving the thorny branches of the thickets with his hands, he let the sharpened brush scrape bloodied lines on his face and hands. He came to the park and walked further until he stood below the high bridge that crossed the river to the other city.

Brad examined the rapids flowing over boulders in the shallow water. Down river, to the south, he could see a dark mass of cliffs though not clearly in such a downpour. He could not see the trees atop the cliffs and the mist of rain and fog obstructed his view. A flow of cars rumbled over the bridge as thousands of people came home from work in the Metro fifty miles away. He gazed up river and did not see the large hydroelectric dam at all. Far below him the water ran strong and he could hear the loud tuss-tap-tussing of the rainfall on the river. He focused, mesmerized, not thinking. A chill from the wet head traveled his body. Brad stepped backwards, tripping first on a long tuft of yellowing grass. Stumbling, he then tripped his left leg on his "sword," plowing his shoulder into the softening dark earth.

The skin beneath the clothing layers felt clammy and wrinkled. A creepy tingling sensation excited Brad's brain looking back at itself. The wind chilled his head and he began a mad shivering twitch.

As the light faded in the premature black shadow made by the clouds, Brad heard the reassuring command, GO. He returned using the same trail, scratching even more of his face; he found himself walking in the downtown.

Passing two blocks of brick fronted stores on the wet, crumbling sidewalk, Brad meandered until he looked up and saw a warm-looking neon sign. He opened the door and stepped inside and among green plants and the polished log framing he heard a woman's voice.

"Brad? Brad Kalna?" a woman wearing a red and black rain jacket said as she came up to him. "How are you doing Brad?" She asked him, looking at Brad's scratched face.

"I'm doing good," he said, unable to recognize this lady. In brilliant perception he could hear the espresso machine as though it gurgled in his head.

"How is your mother doing?" the lady asked. "We had dinner with her and your father when Tom and I went down to the cities, oh, two or three months ago. Poor woman, she's a country girl. I can't believe she moved down there. But you're still living up here, she said." The woman talked longer in order to gauge Brad's condition.

"Yeah."

"Well, I'll have to call your mother and tell her

I saw you," she said. The young lady inside the kitchen set a foam cup on the counter. "Is that mine?" the lady asked the waitress. The woman behind the counter nodded. The woman wearing the raincoat picked up the latte and said one last thing to Brad as she took her drink. "If you need any help, Brad, you remember where I live and my name is in the phone book under Tom and Dotty."

Brad with blithe awareness shook his head as Dotty then exited the shop. Brad stood behind a man donning a full leather duster and cowboy hat. He had ordered and Brad could hear the espresso machine and the lite music playing from the speakers in the corners. Both blared into his mind.

When the gurgling stopped, the skinny woman behind the counter gave the man his drink. "Here's your mocha, Pete." The man set it on the counter to pull money from his wallet.

"Mocha," Brad said in a small whisper. "Mocha?" The echo of the former gurgling and steaming of the espresso machine replayed in his ear. "Moch." He muttered louder. "Moch!" he yelled this time.

Brad reached under his unbuttoned coat and yanked on the knot of the string. His "sword" slid under the coat and fell. It made a wooden "TWANG!" on the wood floor. Brad bent down and grabbed the "sword." He paused while he looked intently at both his hands around the "hilt." He burst upright with the "sword" held high above his head as the tip battered the metal chandelier, causing a swirl of light to circle the room.

The customer in the duster and hat stepped back. "Whoa, there, big fella," he said.

The punk rock-out worker behind the counter

moved back to the safety of the kitchen.

All within a second or two, Brad charged with two giant steps toward his dreaded enemy, "Count Moch," the cup of coffee, steamed milk, chocolate, and whipped cream. With a tremendous and inaccurate blow, the sword cracked hard on the counter, missing the red and blue cardboard cup. The "sword" split with the wood grain. Undeterred, Brad used the shortened "sword" and swiped the black and white marble counter until he whacked the coffee cup into the corner. Coffee, hot chocolate milk, and whipped cream sprayed all over the wall. Brad stood there and the customer wearing the cowboy hat looked calm but stunned.

"You okay, partner?" Pete asked.

Brad dropped the shaft of the stick and pulled open the door, ringing a bell he had not had heard before. YOU HAVE SUCCEEDED. YOU ARE NOW A FRIAR OF THE BROTHERHOOD OF THE WAY! VICTORIOUS! GLORIOUS!

In the street Brad ran in front of a car which squealed as it stopped. Brad ran and entered a door with a small round window. He found himself inside a bar among the happy hour crowd of 7 or 8 people.

Brad shuffled to the men's room. Looking into the mirror, his hair drenched, his face tore up, Brad stared into his own, thought-less eyes. Nervous and excited, he giggled. The small, restrained laugh became a silent fit.

When Brad walked out of the rest room, he scooted to the bar where he ordered a tap beer.

Brad unfolded a dollar from his fold of bills as the short bartender poured him a glass.

A man wearing a brown coat and hat backed

into Brad. The man said nothing and Brad sneered.

He sat on the stool, wedging his forehead into the crook of his left hand. He felt like passing out and his head swayed and bobbed on the fulcrum of the elbow. The bartender and the other patrons observed him, glancing brief glimpses. When 7 PM sounded the last call for happy hour all but two people sitting at the main bar had left the tavern.

The jukebox quit as the television showed the cable news. Brad finished the rest of his beer then ordered another.

Sitting back at the table with his eyes closed, Brad heard the door open. Opening his eyes, seeing a tall police officer. The officer talked with the bartender while she glanced over at Brad. Brad stood and moved quickly toward the rest room.

He disappeared in the entryway to the emergency exit, hearing the officer shout, "Hold it!" Brad plunged both hands into the door and pushed it open.

Brad could hear the policeman talk into the radio microphone clipped to his shoulder board. Brad ran fast, reliving moments from his senior year of track in the 800 meter run. He sloshed through the puddles the alley. At the end of it, he turned right and ran down the hill to the main street. Across the street, he ran down into a lower-level parking lot behind the post office.

Brad tried to hide in the dark corner of some sculpturesque items around the corner. Brad heard the officer's steps and he also saw the beam of the flashlight search the metal and wood forms of junk and art. A police car followed the officer into the lower level parking lot, the squad's searchlight scanning the area.

Brad tried making himself disappear, pinning his shoulders to the white-washed wall. The policeman on foot walked past Brad a few steps. When the officer turned, his flashlight beam shined onto Brad's face, blinding the Friar Brother-errant.

"I've got him," the officer called into his radio. The other officer in the car exited the vehicle and approached so that the two police men cornered Brad beneath the twirling blades of seven foot metal wind mill.

"Brad! Brad Kalna!" one officer said. "Your mother called us. Someone told her you might be in trouble."

Brad said nothing but his body shook and he stared from one officer to the other.

"We need to get you some help, Brad," the other officer said.

Finally able to speak, Brad shouted, "I just want to go home, but I don't know where that is!"

"We'll take you there," the second officer said.

"I don't know where to go! I don't know where I belong!"

"Come with us and you're on the way there before you know it," the first officer said.

"The Way," Brad whispered. "The Way!" he yelled. "You'll show me the Way!"

"Yeah," the second officer said. "Come on. Just walk slowly out of the corner."

THE WAY. THE WAY. THE WAY.

Brad smiled as he moved out from beneath the spinning windmill.

In a Time That Pi Forgot

I was born on Armistice Day, nineteen-hundred and seventy-three, to Jonathan S. and Maureen Kielty in Oz, Utopia. My mother was a housewife and a part-time lunchroom helper at a nearby elementary school. Her Uncle Flannigan, whom she never knew, died in August 1918 during the Argonne offensive. She knew the significance of my birthday from the stories of my grandmother who turned twelve the day her parents received the news. I was actually born within minutes of the armistice that ended the Great Big Kindermord. I was nine minutes and some odd seconds late on that particular day. My mother called me her Great War because she labored 18 hours to get me "the hell out," as she would put it. My aunty, who was a nurse in the delivery room, said that at around twenty minutes after eleven, my mother bellowed like a cannon.

My mother, with her half Irish smile, grinned, prayed, screamed, cursed, threatened, and all together bore the pain. And she did so for a lot of years. Between my age of 17 and 25 she gave forth her empathy and her sympathy. In her reflections on my life and my problems, Mom once said that I reminded her of her uncle who died in the war against fascism. He was in Italy and, the story goes, stepped on a landmine. Great Uncle Lou apparently had been quite a writer. My grandma has even shown me some of his stories and a few of the letters he sent home. They are all very interesting pieces of literature, and they all struck me as though written by gifted madman.

My father, of unknown adopted stock, named me Pi after his favorite concept--a mathematical constant that had no end, or at least any known end. Growing up he always told me, "Son, your name has no end." I didn't quite understand that concept until I learned it much later in school. About age 9 I asked my mother why I had no middle name like my older sisters and older brother. "If spelled out, Pi, your name is long enough." And still, the concept of Pi puzzles and bewilders me. How precise can a string of numbers get?

I grew up in a house of much love. With such a large family in a five-bedroom house we each lived in one another's face. By the time I was 7 my siblings began to leave the house. The last two sisters left when I was 13. Over the next six years a couple of them came back to stay and make things easier in their lives, but those were only transient stays

Growing up our only bathroom had no lock. Since I was the youngest child (a full six years behind the next closest one) I had no concept of privacy and had free access to the bathroom until I was about five. I hated bathing for the most part, so most of the time my sisters would fill up a bubble bath. I still have pictures of those events. I guess I found a tub of suds quite fun.

Potty training was a terrible experience for me. And I do remember that whole experience. No matter what type of business I had with the vestibule I remember feeling the sincere need to take off all my clothes before I went so that I didn't have an accident and get them soiled. I don't particularly recall how long I felt the need to disrobe, but I remember not wanting to take a dump at the elementary school in kindergarten or first grade. Since then I have had an honest liking for my own bathroom when I have to attend to such business.

Indeed, I would have been highly embarrassed, and received much criticism from my peers, if I had to undress in the stall at grade school. Yet, I did get into quite an embarrassing situation in kindergarten when I found a little wood tick on the end of my pecker. He was stuck, really stuck well, but I got him off. The rumor, unfortunately, spread around the bathroom and eventually into the hall. I felt so dumb when the teacher, Mrs. Hillary, walked part way into the boy's lavatory to ask if my thing was ok.

Not all of my childhood experiences had such a comic twist. I remember--well, I think it was just after I left diapers to sleep in training pants--getting out of my crib one morning as usual by crawling out over the side and dexterously scaling down to the floor. I went down the stairs and yelled for my mother. "Ma?" I yelled. "Ma?" I repeated. "Dad? DAD!" No one answered. For some reason I knew for a fact that my mother was not around. So, I screamed for my dad some more. I went to my parent's room and looked out the window facing the driveway. I saw my dad in his Mustang driving from right to left down the hill along our curved driveway. I began to cry as he partially disappeared behind apple trees and thickets, dropping below the hill and completely out of sight. That was a horrible fear of terror. I cried furiously and I shat in my footed pajamas. Yeah, that was an icky feeling all around, besides on my leg. Surprisingly, today I still suffer from a slight incontinence every couple of years due to my medicine and my diet, and the feeling of abandonment lingers with me to this day. Just another powerful memory recall.

I had a few other scary experiences when I was young. The dreams my active imagination conjured began at that time. Although I don't know when the last vision of sleep will come, I do remember pretty much when it started.

I always stayed up late with my mother while she waited for my father to come home from his second shift job. As a result, I became an early fan of the late movies. To this day I greatly enjoy film. My early favorites were those old melodramatic monster movies starring Boris Karloff and, of course, Bela Lugosi.

While four years old I had a nightmare about the Grand Vamp. I didn't have much of a clue about dreams, what they're for, what they say, and why we have them. But sleeping in my warm cozy bed, which I shared with my older brother, I dreamt I was sleeping in the back of our Winnebago on the folding table that made into a bed. I knew I was alone in the motor home. I looked to my right, and yep, up stepped Dracula into the camper. He looked exactly like Bela--the bestest--did in the original movie: portending of the dark, evil, not-dead, sucker of life-giving blood and virgin innocence. Dracula stood by the door up by the cab for a few minutes. He pulled his cape up around his lower face with the left tuxedoed arm. With those wild, hypnotic eyes, in uniform black and white and bloodshot, he acknowledged that he saw me. After nodding with that pale blue part of his face, popping out the top above his arm, Dracula took one step toward the back of the Winnebago--toward me. Thankfully, I woke up.

Unthankfully, I had the same dream two or three years later. This time, Dracula made it past the point when I woke up the first time. All the while, as he walked toward me with his left arm up, still holding his cape and hiding his fangs, I looked into those eyes and said, "Well, I don't like this at all."

I remember that I really wished I could wake up. But it was too late. Dracula loomed above me. He pulled his left arm away from his mouth (revealing his razor sharp teeth), drawing the cape back behind him and looming over the counter top above the bed. The right arm, outstretched, with the usual cape histrionics, hung over my legs. He leaned over. His face was about a foot from mine. I don't remember what his breath smelled like other than the smell of death. Up close, and especially in the dreamy nighttime when you can see everything, his death mask spoke one message to me: "You, Pi, are doomed."

The Bridge

"I hope Dale's ready. We're already gonna be late," said Tim to John as they sat down in the truck bed next to the canoe.

John's dad drove the old county road M to the part of the town on the plateau south of the railroad tracks. When they pulled into Dale's driveway, Dale ran out of the house dressed like the other two boys in trunks, T-shirt, and sneakers, and carrying a canvas bag.

John's dad drove to the boat landing below the bridge connecting Wisconsin to Minnesota. Anxious to start the adventure, the boys undid the ropes and jabbered while they unloaded the canoe, setting it on the sand halfway in the water. They loaded the cooler and Dale's canvas bag, two oars and three life jackets. Before the boys shoved off, John's dad said, "You boys be careful. You're twelve now, so don't do anything stupid. You got change for the phone call?"

"Yeah, Dad."

"Be careful," John's dad said as a last warning as Tim helped Dale push the boat off the sand.

Tim, who sat in the middle, gave the order, "Left full rudder. All ahead full."

"Ah, shut up," John said. All three boys laughed, excited at their first journey down the river without adults. "Is he still there?" John asked about his father.

"Yep, he just waved." Tim said.

The high sandstone bluff that loomed over downtown Osceola dominated the Wisconsin shoreline. Scrub trees grew outward from the sides of the erosion-scaled mini-terraces of the dark yellow sandstone. On the Minnesota side, the boys moved leisurely past the last tip of the long peninsula that followed the river to form the county park. People swam at the sandy beach. Even for a late June Saturday morning, the air already had a scorching warm touch. With no clouds above, the water reflected the sun so the surface looked like a bright white, slightly wavy mirror.

"Stop rowing so fast you guys. Let's just drift. We got all day," Tim said in his commanding way. Dale stopped paddling, then John slowed his pace. Once the canoe passed the last part of the bluffs, swamps and marsh separated the riverbanks from the rolling tall hills on either side.

The river was full of canoes and boats. People were escaping the heat with a day on the St. Croix. In previous summers, the boys had spent time on the river on day trips or camp outings with John's parents or Dale's father. For centuries, millennia perhaps, the river had flowed in its twisting course, changing its shape and direction, sinking deeper into the earth, channeling its imprint for the future, forming the entire broad valley to mark its life.

Dale rummaged through his canvas bag and pulled out a pack of cigarettes, handing them and a green lighter back to Tim. Tim lit up. "Want one, John?" he asked after exhaling, holding the pack and the lighter behind his head. John lit one and puffed several times, quite aware of the buzz in his head. When Dale finally got his smokes back, he lit one as well, and the boys just sat in the boat enjoying the dizzying lightheadedness.

"Boy, does this feel good," said John.

"Yeah, but my dad says the effect doesn't last once you begin to smoke regularly."

"You didn't tell him you were smoking, did you?" Tim asked.

"Well, yeah."

"You idiot," he said, "he'll tell our parents. If my mom and Gary found out they'd ground me for two months."

"Don't worry." Dale, slightly intimidated, assured the other two his drunken dad did not care too much about what they did.

As the canoe moved through a curve in the channel, the tall green grass on the shore and the trees on the banks receded and the boys could see a drawbridge made with the same materials as railroad ties, heavy beams oiled dark to protect them against the corrosion of weather and water. A skeleton of beams suspended the bridge, and a large circular block of concrete held it at the center. On this concrete block, the bridge once twisted through gears to allow boats to pass, but now the gears were rusted.

"When do you think the bridge last moved?" Dale asked.

"Who knows?" said John.

"Who cares?" retorted Tim.

Further down river past the draw bridge, Dale, Tim, and John could see the sandbars exposed by the closing of the dam in St. Croix Falls. Hordes of people picnicked or swam here. Kids ran all over in the hot summer mayhem as the boys passed under the bridge. Dale, looking over the side said, "The water's deep here." Once to the sandbar, they dragged the canoe half out of the water and unloaded it. All at the same time, the boys removed their T-shirts and sprawled out on beach towels.

"Hey, Dale," John motioned to him to look at his legs, "you're getting pretty burnt." The tops of his thighs indeed looked red and burnt. Taking some sun block from his canvas bag, he applied it to his body, handing the bottle to Tim next.

"Bastard," John called Tim, "you took it all. Dale, you got anymore?"

"No," he said, shaking his head.

The boys gored on the sandwiches and chips and the soda they brought with them.

"Good sandwiches," Dale exclaimed. The other two agreed.

The boys centered their attention on two college-age girls sun bathing in bikinis.

"Hey, guys, let's jump off the bridge," said Tim, breaking the trance.

"I don't know, guys. Sounds kind of dangerous," said Dale, chiming caution.

"Come on. Don't be a pussy," Tim said.

"Don't press him, Tim. If he doesn't want to do it, it's okay."

"No way. One goes or two go, we all go. You'll be all right, Dale. Just come with us."

"If he doesn't want to, we can't make him."

"Don't worry. There's nothing to worry about, Dale."

"All right," he replied a moment later.

"Great," Tim said as he jumped up, grabbing his shirt and towel.

The boys packed up everything and paddled back upstream. They landed the canoe on the Minnesota shore near the base of the concrete abutment. They agreed to leave on their shoes while they walked the trestle. Scampering up the steep embankment, they stood at the end of the bridge between the railroad tracks and looked down the semi-cave-like length interspersed with shadows from the wooden skeletal superstructure. The water on this end, they could clearly see, looked too shallow for jumping. Tim asked, "Dale, you said the water was deeper on the Wisconsin side."

"It's okay there," Dale said.

Tim took the first step onto the trestle, looking down to cadence his step so that his feet fell on the beams and not in the wide spaces between them. John looked at Dale. Dale took one look down at the water. Looking hesitant, he gulped and followed Tim who, at an arrogant pace, had advanced ten yards.

"We should probably swim to the Wisconsin side once we jump." John said.

"Nonsense," replied Tim, "the river's not moving that fast. We can swim back to the boat."

Three-quarters of the way across, Tim stopped and looked north upriver. Then he looked south, holding his hips with his hands. Dale and John duly arrived at the spot. John looked at the sand bar, still full of frolickers. Dale looked straight down at the clean river water. A stream of foam moved fast with the current.

"Well, you chickens can cop out. I'm going ahead," said Tim, stepping up to the edge with his feet on two separate beams.

"Remember Dale, you don't have to go with us," John said.

"No. . . I'll come."

"READY!" Tim shouted. "YE-HAWWW!" The people on the sand bar heard the shrill sound. They looked at the bridge, saw Dale jump, then John jump and hang a moment in the air before falling feet first into the water.

When Dale's head came up, Tim and John had begun swimming for the canoe. The river was comparatively narrow here. But the current moved at a swifter pace than boys realized. Now following the other two, Dale said, "Hell if that bastard is gonna call me chicken pussy." As he spoke water trickled into his mouth. He coughed and spit.

All the time, the current carried the boys downstream from the bridge. Dale's shoes felt heavy now. It was harder to kick. He struggled in the water. Halfway to the shore, perhaps thirty-five yards away, he began to panic.

"HELP! TIM! JOHN! HELP!" he yelled.

John could see Dale barely above the water line. "Tim! Get the canoe. I'm going back for him." John, kicked off his shoes to speed swim back toward the middle of the river.

"Hurry, John, he's going under!" Tim yelled from shore, exhausted from his hard swim.

Now John, too, began to tire as he swam to reach his friend. Finally he reached him, just when Dale choked on swallowed water. "Just relax, Dale. Relax. I got you." He put his arm under Dale's, wrapped it tightly around the Dale's chest, and swam toward the shore. "Come on. I need you to help me, Dale! Keep swimming!"

"I can't, John. My feet are too heavy. My shoes...my shoes..."

"Kick them off. Just try and float. That's all you have to do."

Swimming on his side using his right arm and huge scissor kicks, John moved closer to the shore. He could see Tim paddling the canoe toward them as fast as he could but having trouble keeping the boat pointed straight. "Hurry, Tim! I'm getting cramps!" Either Tim had to reach them or they needed to get to shore. "Keep at it, Dale. Keep kicking. We're almost there." Thirteen yards. Ten. Six. Just when John had nothing left to give, he felt the ground with his bare feet, two yards from shore. He pulled Dale onto the sand.

Tim arrived in the canoe and jumped out. "You guys all right?" he asked.

Dale and John could not speak. They both breathed large gasps of air and spit out water.

"Boy," Tim said, "are we lucky."

"It wasn't luck," Dale said, spitting again. "It was John."

Brothers

When I was real young, probably just beginning
grade school, my brother made a small wooden
box in his high school shop class. It was made of
varnished white pine, perhaps four inches wide,
three inches tall and seven inches long. One small
piece of pine was laid across the center so that it
actually had two compartments almost entirely
square in area. He kept the box in our bedroom on
our dresser. When he left for college I inherited the
room and practically everything he didn't take with
him, including the box. Over the years I used the
box, mostly as an ornament but sometimes to hold
little mementos and various trinkets that I acquired
in high school, college, and afterwards.

About six or seven years ago I tried to return

the box. After all, it was his. He look at me as I proudly held out the box for him to take back. I thought to impress him that I kept it all those years. Scoffingly, he looked at me and said that he didn't want it. Quite honestly, I felt offended. I always looked up to my brother and he seemed to regard the box as some piece of garbage which time discarded from his sentiments.

My brother and I, most likely because he was ten years older, never had a close relationship. However, like all true things (family among them) my brother was at my side during terribly desperate moments. And since all human gratitude stands feebly next to the deeds others do for a person, even lifesaving deeds, I owe him great debts. I probably owe him as much as I owe anyone. I can never repay the things that Victor did for me, although I tried by returning his box.

Not long ago I sat at my desk in my room one night, resting silently in my chair trying to clear my head from months of recent stress. The box caught my sight as it rested on the lower level of my bookshelf. Then I thought, "What if he wanted you to keep the box." I smiled, even though it had taken me so long to "get it." Perhaps, brothers giving love to brothers is itself the best reward. With no doubt he has given me more than an old, worn out pine box. At one point he gave me some hope in a hopeless time. Thanks, Vic. Love, your brother, Pi.

Beneath in the Underworld

The Lord Christ Jesus descended briefly into the depths of hell, a journey he sometimes makes to set Justice right. He approached the Great Hall of the Evil Council through the gardens of poisoned vines blooming sour grapes. Without movement or word or any effort whatsoever, the Lord compelled the two legged serpent standing as sergeant at arms to open the gate of the hall and the Savior of all mankind entered the porch.

Two sentinel beasts approached with wicked weapons raised and crossed to bar his path, and then suddenly the demons dropped their evil spears to the stone floor and placed their flesh rotten hands over their eyes and fell next to their guard arms. They lay writhing, immobilized by the light of Truth emanating from Christ and suffered pain more severe than that which they inflicted on others in the ancient death hole of their kingdom.

Jesus sent forth lightning from his eyes and the whole of the unholy hell trembled as the sound of righteous fury emanated while the bolts of Love struck the doors to the antechamber banquet hall. The doors of mighty twisted and demented wormwood exploded inward on a table of devils feasting on a fresh harvest of suicide, crushing the minioned men-snakes under the weight of their own iniquitous lumber.

And into the great room of ghastly decor walked Christ shone in the bright raiment of redemption that illuminated in the brilliant glory of God, the Father.

While the demons suffered from the Truth in their presence, the thing their hate hated most, Satan staggeringly rose from the head table along the far wall under the tapestry of his doomly principality.

"What reason do you intrude on our supper, oh Son of Man?"

"I have come to reclaim one wrongly committed to your possession, Prince of Lies and Earl of Evil."

"Once again, your pestilent Father breaks his own laws, for he said that the mortally sinned belong to us as meat on our table to dine and fill our bellies with His failures."

"The Father neither makes nor breaks laws, Satan. He is the law. And he has thus decreed that you may not devour this one, an innocent victim like the others of your falsehoods, driven mad with a soul poison unleashed by wicked servants in one of their evil wars."

Jesus then descended the six steps to the main floor of the banquet hall and raised his left arm and waved from his right side across his pure and loving heart, casting on the gluttonous dinner guests a foul feeling in their stomachs. And they spewed their meal on the hot stone floor. The remains of the meal gathered in a whirlwind from the Lord's slightly blowing breath and piled on a stone tile that Jesus set aside.

The Lord commanded, "Rise," and a whole man suddenly rose from the pile of remains and he was clothed in white silk and he held an aura so bright as to look blue.

Satan stood suffering and powerless before the Lord and the man that Christ saved. The scales of the underworld master's face became as flushed red as red-hot can get and he swilled his saliva in his mouth with anger.

"For this insolence, Nazarene, I shall unleash ten times still the horror on your flock."

"Stand not over confident, Mephisto-devil, for a shepherd always awake never sleeps. Mark your time for I, the raptured spirit, shall protect them. And worse for you still, for I shall drag all your domain and dispossess you of all your ability, and then I shall bring all before the Judgment of the Lord on a day of the Father's choosing. You will be bound and cast into the Lake of Fire, burning in the fuel of brimstone ignited by an explosion of universal peace. Your planned reign grows short at the passing moment. Mark your time, Lucifer."

The redeemed man who once was demon fodder looked lovingly at Christ, and with thanks for his redemption.

Jesus said, "Come, Brian. Your Father awaits you."

And together they ascended the six steps and

walked through the battered doorway and into the porch and out the gate, past the garden of future bitter wine and left hell for the Peace of Heaven.

ABOUT THE AUTHOR

Who is Pi Kielty? That is the question many people have. Where does he live? What does he do? What is he like?

There may never be satisfactory answers to these and the other questions that people may want to know. In fact, does Pi know these answers himself? Perhaps not.

Pi Kielty has written stories since college, without much success or acclaim. He has been published in only one magazine, as far as we know, "weird stuff."

www.ingramcontent.com/pod-product-compliance
Lightning Source LLC
Chambersburg PA
CBHW020330130626
46549CB00003B/1111